Living and Nonliving in the Mountains

T0101170

Rebecca Rissman

Heinemann LIBRARY
Chicago, Illinois

© 2014 Heinemann Library
an imprint of Capstone Global Library, LLC
Chicago, Illinois

To contact Capstone Global Library please phone 800-747-4992, or visit our website www.capstonepub.com

All rights reserved. No part of this publication may be reproduced or transmitted in any form or by any means, electronic or mechanical, including photocopying, recording, taping, or any information storage and retrieval system, without permission in writing from the publisher.

Edited by Daniel Nunn, Rebecca Rissman, and Catherine Veitch
Designed by Cynthia Della-Rovere
Picture research by Tracy Cummins
Production by Sophia Argyris
Originated by Capstone Global Library Ltd

ISBN 978-1-4109-5385-8 (hc)
ISBN 978-1-4109-5392-6 (pb)

Library of Congress Cataloging-in-Publication Data

Rissman, Rebecca.
Living and nonliving in the mountains / Rebecca Rissman. pages cm.—(Is it living or nonliving?)
Includes bibliographical references and index.
ISBN 978-1-4109-5385-8 (hb)—ISBN 978-1-4109-5392-6 (pb) 1. Mountains—Juvenile literature. 2. Life (Biology)—Juvenile literature. I. Title.

QH87.R57 2013
577.5'3—dc23

Acknowledgments
We would like to thank the following for permission to reproduce photographs: Getty Images pp. 14 (© Joseph Van Os), 18 (© Klaus Nigge); Shutterstock pp. 1, 21 (© Christopher Boswell), 4, 23a (© Rigucci), 5 (© Standa Riha), 6 (© Eduard Kyslynskyy), 7 (© Ekaterina Pokrovsky), 8, 23d (© Galyna Andrushko), 9, 23c (© Jiri Vavricka), 10 (© Popova Valeriya), 11, 23b (© µ), 12 (© Paul Aniszewski), 13 (© Sergey Toronto), 15 (© Dennis Donohue), 16 (© SergeyIT), 17 (© Joel Whitaker), 19 (© Wendy Nero), 20 (© Asaf Eliason), 21 (©Christopher Boswell), 22 (© pixy).

Front cover photograph of a mountain goat with kid in Utah reproduced with permission of Superstock (© Animals Animals).

We would like to thank Michael Bright and Nancy Harris for their invaluable help in the preparation of this book.

Every effort has been made to contact copyright holders of material reproduced in this book. Any omissions will be rectified in subsequent printings if notice is given to the publisher.

All the Internet addresses (URLs) given in this book were valid at the time of going to press. However, due to the dynamic nature of the Internet, some addresses may have changed, or sites may have changed or ceased to exist since publication. While the author and publisher regret any inconvenience this may cause readers, no responsibility for any such changes can be accepted by either the author or the publisher.

Some words are in bold, **like this**.
You can find them in the glossary on page 23.

Printed in the United States 5483

Contents

What Is a Mountain? 4
What Are Living Things? 6
What Are Nonliving Things? 8
Is a Pine Tree Living or Nonliving? 10
Is Ice Living or Nonliving? 12
Is a Mountain Lion Living or Nonliving? 14
Is Soil Living or Nonliving? 16
Is an Eagle Living or Nonliving? 18
Is a Wildflower Living or Nonliving? . . . 20
What Do You Think? *22*
Glossary *23*
Find Out More, Index *24*

What Is a Mountain?

A mountain is a rocky, tall **landform**.

Mountains are very large.

Different types of plants and animals live on the mountains.

There are **nonliving** things in the mountains too.

What Are Living Things?

Living things are alive. Living things need air and **sunlight**. Living things need food and water.

Living things grow and change.

Living things move on their own.

What Are Nonliving Things?

Nonliving things are not alive. Nonliving things do not need air and **sunlight**.

Nonliving things do not need food or water.

Nonliving things do not grow and change on their own.

Nonliving things do not move on their own.

Is a Pine Tree Living or Nonliving?

A pine tree needs water.

A pine tree moves on its own toward the sun.

A pine tree grows and changes.

A pine tree needs air and **sunlight**.

A pine tree is **living**.

Is Ice Living or Nonliving?

Ice does not move on its own.

Ice does not grow.

Ice does not need food.

Ice does not need air or **sunlight**.

Ice is **nonliving**.

Is a Mountain Lion Living or Nonliving?

A mountain lion grows and changes.

A mountain lion needs food and water.

A mountain lion moves on its own.

A mountain lion needs air and **sunlight**.

A mountain lion is **living**.

Is Soil Living or Nonliving?

Soil does not move on its own.

Soil does not need food or water.

Soil does not grow on its own.

Soil does not need air or **sunlight**.

Soil is **nonliving**.

Is an Eagle Living or Nonliving?

An eagle grows and changes.

An eagle needs food and water.

An eagle moves on its own.

An eagle needs air and **sunlight**.

An eagle is **living**.

Is a Wildflower Living or Nonliving?

A wildflower moves on its own toward the sun.

A wildflower needs water.

A wildflower grows and changes.

A wildflower needs air and **sunlight**.

A wildflower is **living**.

What Do You Think?

Is this rock **living** or **nonliving**?

Glossary

landform natural shape in the land

living alive. Living things need food and water. They breathe and move on their own. They grow and change.

nonliving not alive. Nonliving things do not need food and water. They do not move on their own. They do not grow and change on their own.

sunlight light from the sun

Find Out More

Websites

Facthound offers a safe, fun way to find Internet sites related to this book. All of the sites on Facthound have been researched by our staff.

Here's all you do:
Visit www.facthound.com

Type in this code: 9781410953858

Books

Dickmann, Nancy. *Mount Everest (Explorer Tales)*. Chicago: Raintree, 2013.

Lindeen, Carol K. *Living and Nonliving*. Mankato, Minn.: Capstone, 2008.

Waldron, Melanie. *Mountains (Habitat Survival)*. Chicago: Raintree, 2013.

Index

eagle 18–19
food and water 6, 10, 14, 18, 20
ice 12–13
landform 4, 23
living things 6–7, 10–11, 14–15, 18–21, 23
mountain lion 14–15
nonliving things 8–9, 12–13, 16–17, 23
pine tree 10–11
rock 22
soil 16–17
sunlight 6, 11, 15, 19, 21, 23
wildflower 20–21